Topics

Blood vessels....

Heart...

Waste Removal....

Hi friends, my name is Halle the Heart, and today we are going to learn about the circulatory system!

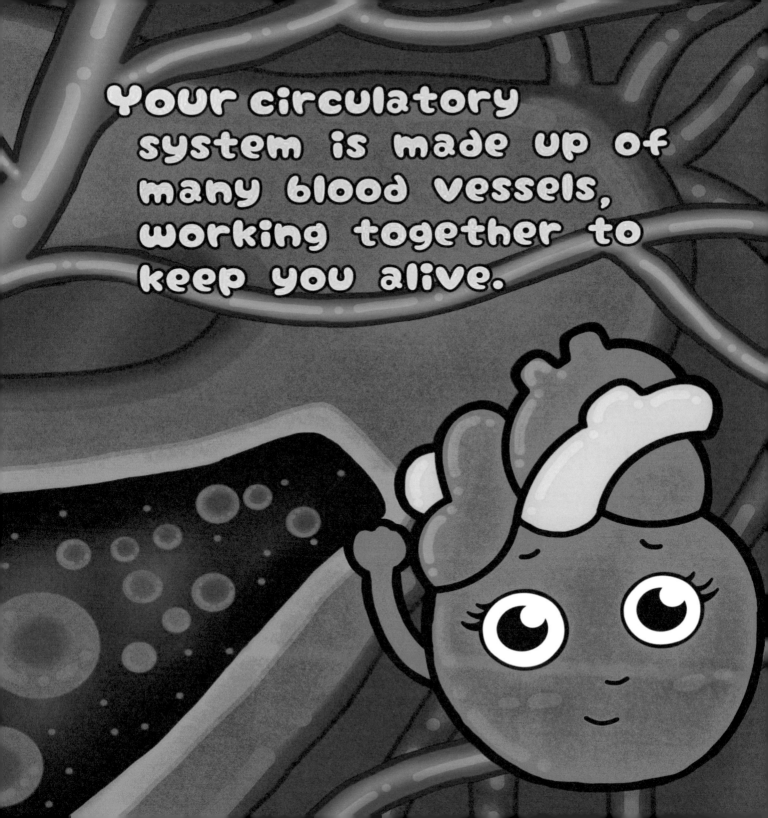

Your circulatory system is made up of many blood vessels, working together to keep you alive.

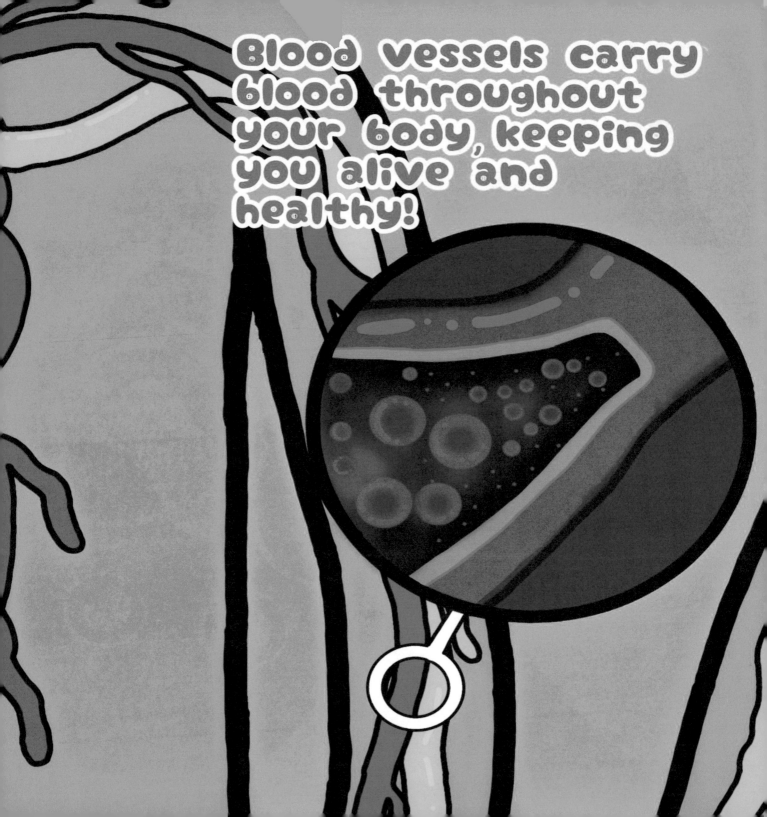

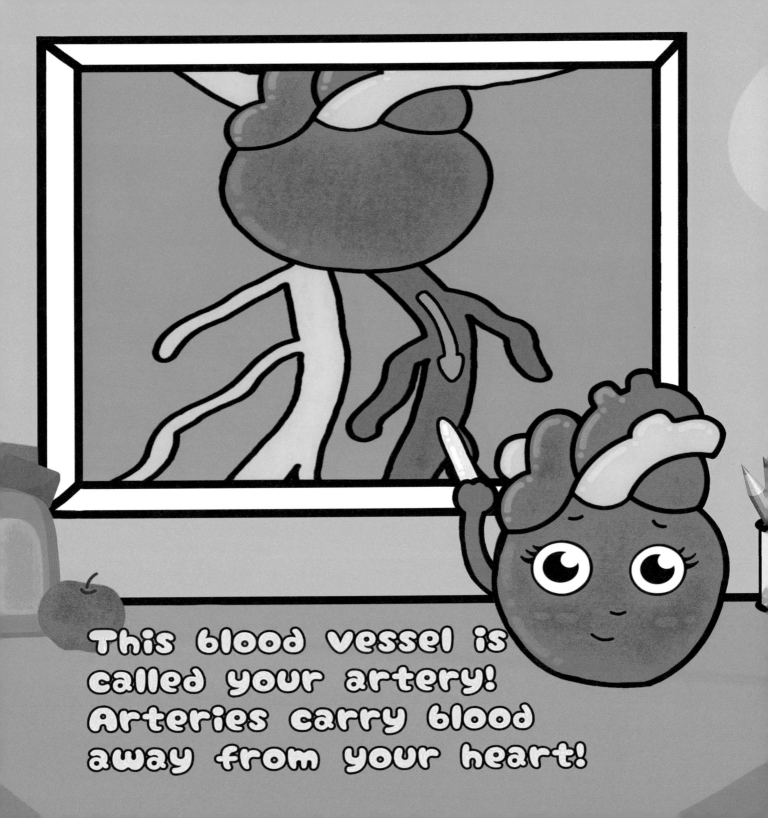

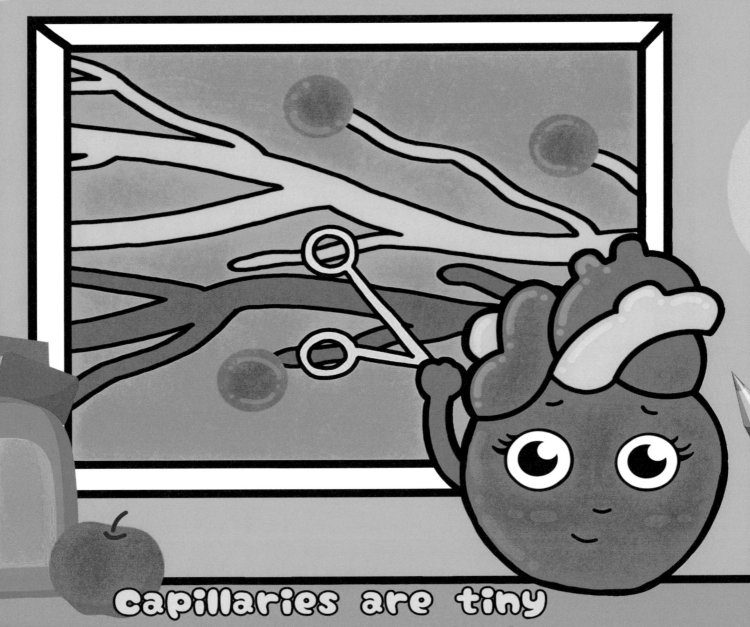

Capillaries are tiny blood vessels that carry blood to your body cells!

Blood is a liquid that carries things through your body. Let's look closer!

Your blood carries many things throughout your blood vessels. This is called a nutrient.

Nutrients are found in the foods you eat!

Your circulatory system carries these nutrients...

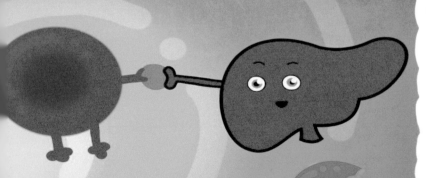

to your organs and muscles...

to make you big and strong!

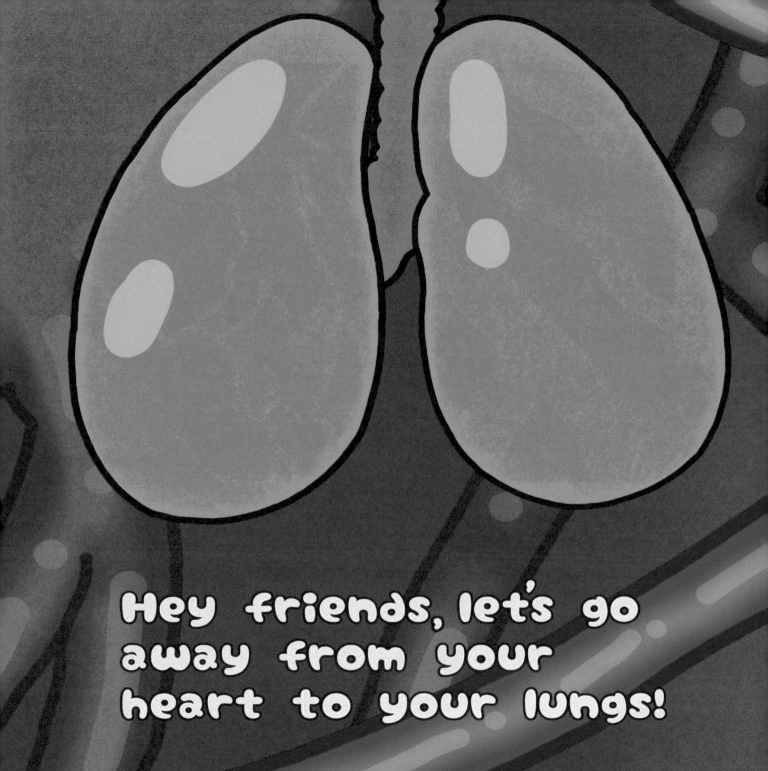

When you breathe in (inhale), your lungs take oxygen from the air around you!

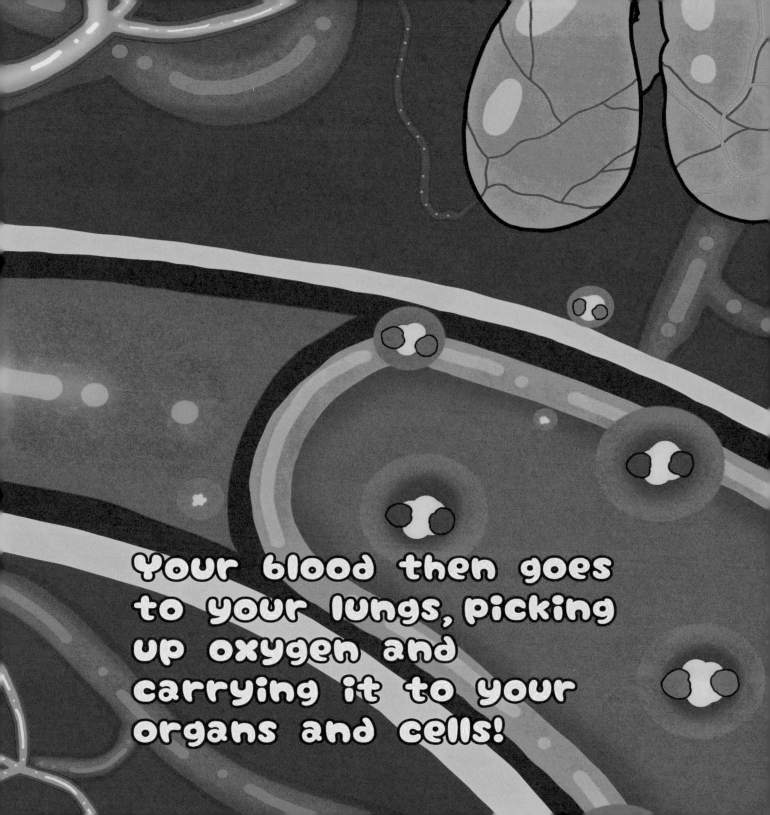

Your blood then goes to your lungs, picking up oxygen and carrying it to your organs and cells!

Let's bring oxygen to your heart! Do you remember which vessel carries blood towards the heart?

Good job! See friends, organs like our heart needs oxygen because it gives them energy to keep us alive.

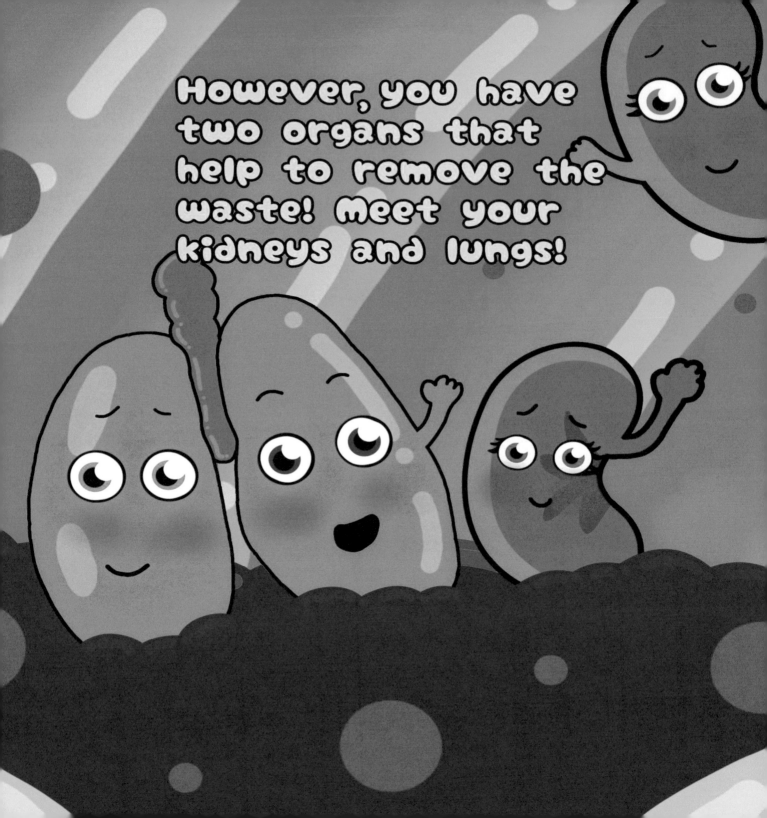

Your blood picks up waste throughout your body..

and brings it to your kidneys! Kidneys then remove...

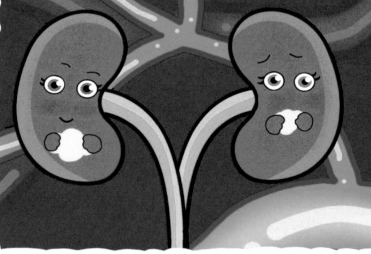

Waste by a process...

called urinating, also known as peeing!

Let's learn another way how your circulatory system removes waste from your body.

Car

Bun

Die

Ox

Hide

Carbon Dioxide

Hey friends, do you want to learn a cool word?

Carbon dioxide exits your lungs when you breathe out (exhale).

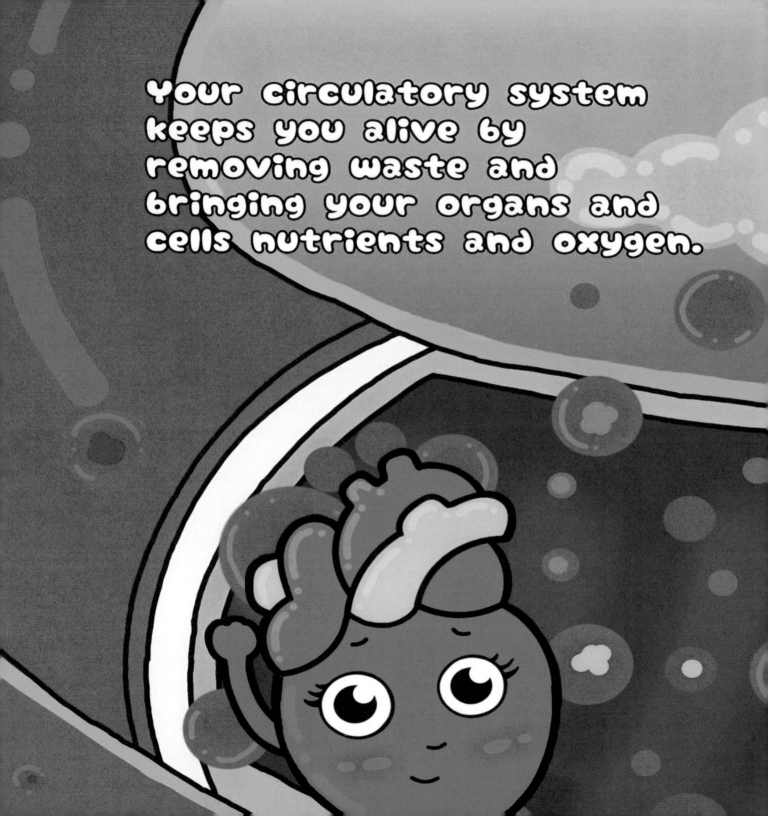

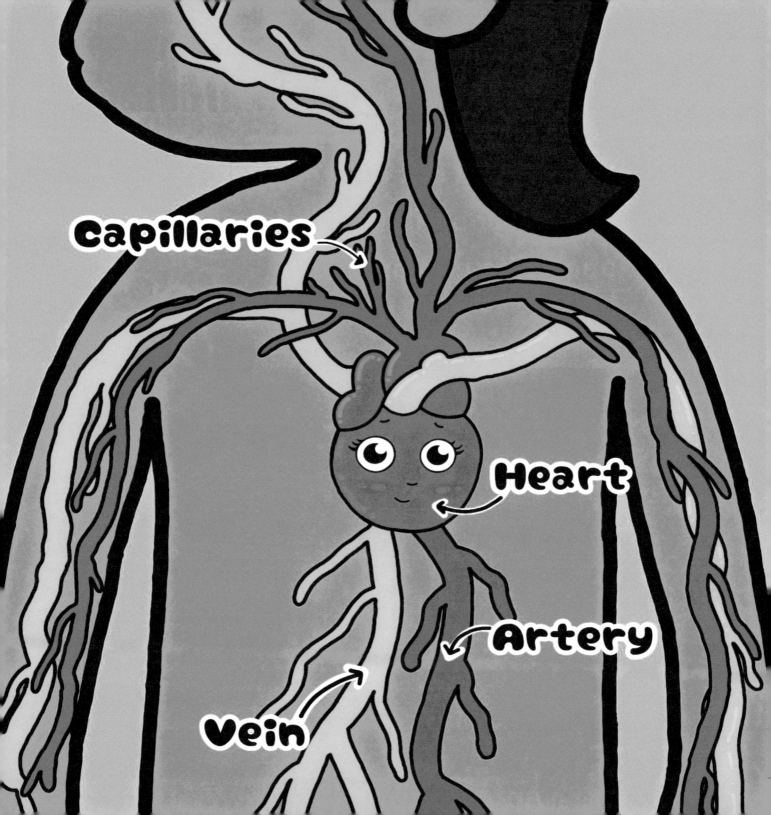

Hey! Check out our respiratory system book to learn more about the human body!

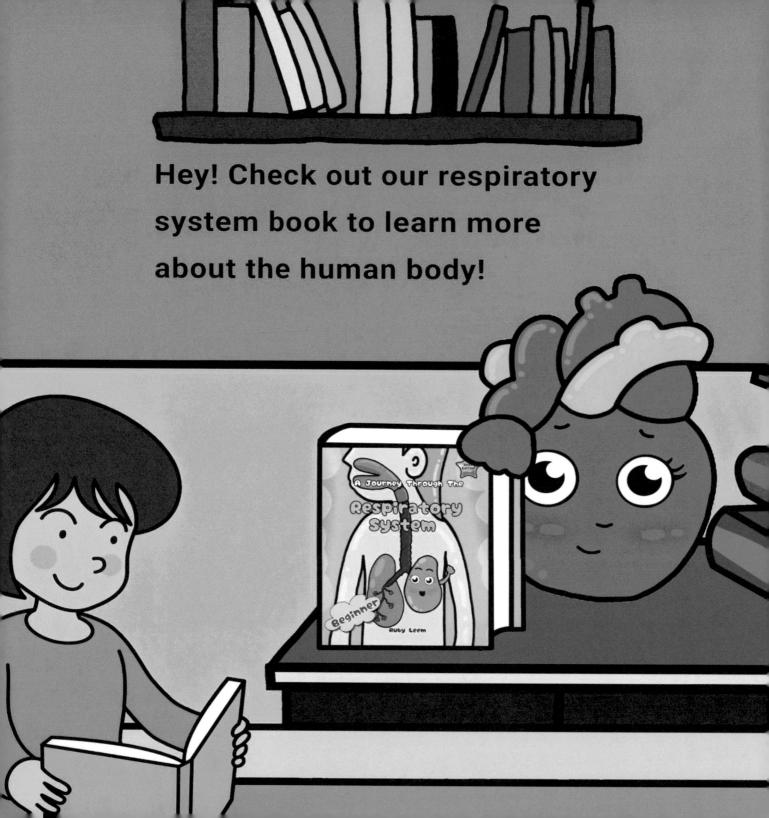

Rubyleem.com

Check out our website for freebies and more

We would love if you could leave us a review on Amazon !

Don't forget to check out our Planet Earth series!

Made in United States
Troutdale, OR
11/20/2024

25084439R00021